The Business of Hair
An Entrepreneurs Perspective

Chris Chaney
Copyright © 2020 Chris Chaney
All rights reserved.
ISBN: 9798680674352

Contents

1). Introduction/Disclaimer (Pg 4)

2). Chapter One: The Genesis (Pg 7)

3). Chapter Two: Let's Talk About Business (Pg 13)

4). Chapter Three: Your Team (Pg 34)

5). Chapter Four: Your Advisors (Pg 39)

6). Chapter Five: Mentors (Pg 46)

7). Conclusion (Pg 49)

8). Acknowledgement (Pg 52)

Dedication:

This book is dedicated to my dad. He was my model for my state board exam, and he was the first head that I cut in the shop. Unfortunately, he wasn't able to see our shop open or witness its growth. He passed a few months before our grand opening. He always believed in my potential and made sure to let me know how proud he was to be my dad. This book is just a small token of my gratitude for his unwavering faith in my goals.

Introduction/Disclaimer:

"Few people attain great lives, in large part, because it is just so easy to settle for a good life." - Jim Collins, Good to Great: Why Some Companies Make the Leap... and Others Don't.

I'm Chris. I'm a rapper, turned janitor, turned barbershop owner, and it's been a hell of a journey. As you read or listen to this book, I'd like for you to hear it as a conversation between you and me. I know the title says, The Business of Hair, but the bulk of this book is written with barber overtones. There are keys to success in this book for other hair and beauty industry professionals. For that matter, for anybody in business for themselves. I just don't want you to feel played for me, not mentioning your segment of the industry. Hey, I'm an entrepreneur like you.

The views you'll read or listen to in this book were written from my perspective, laced with research. I'm not writing this book with the assumption that you don't know or don't have access to any of this information.

In contrast, I'm writing this book in an attempt to show you how this information pertains to our industry as a whole. No, this isn't a book on how to build your clientele. You can pick up just about any book from Gary V or Seth Godin for tips on building better brands. However, implementing some of what you'll read or hear in this book could easily attract more business. My goal is to help you paint a picture of your long game in this industry and help build a stronger foundation to get there. With that said, I encourage you to seek a competent professional before implementing anything in this book. In short, run it by them first.

I'm in Arkansas, Fort Smith, to be exact, and every state has its laws on what you may read or hear in this book. If this book helps you or your business in any way, feel free to shoot me an email at chris@cisternamanagement.com or hit me up on Twitter or Instagram @thechrischaney. I hope you enjoy it.

Chapter One: The Genesis:

It was Saturday afternoon and I had spent about three or four hours at my cousin Josh's barbershop. It wasn't unusual for me to show up, spend a few hours, and listen to shop talk. Occasionally, I'd put in my two cents, start a few debates, or I'd listen to the latest sports news. Now, if you know me, you know I'm not into sports for the most part at all. I was on the football team in high school and ran track. Running track was my shit for the record. If I had the choice to watch golf or football, I'd choose golf. Yeah, I'm that guy.

The shop closed at about five, and I stuck around for at least another hour to talk with Josh. We talk about business goals, his shop, and my current projects. We dapped up, he got in his car, I got in mine, and we dipped out, just like that.

As I was riding down the interstate toward my place, I got the craziest idea. I thought, I'm going to barberschool. I called my homeboy Mike and his brother Jesse to run the idea across them. They both said it was a no-brainer and to go for it. Then I called Josh. I said, yo, I think I'm signing up for barberschool. He laughed, mainly because it was a completely random idea that seemed to have come out of nowhere.

Two weeks later, I was enrolled, and one of the most epic journeys in my life had begun. I was 30 plus, self-employed, and starting over. Not because I wasn't doing ok in life financially, but to just start again. It was a career shift. I didn't grow up with the notion that career shifts were ok, so it felt crazy weird going to barberschool.

When it was all said and done, I'd met some pretty dope people in school, a few friends for life, and at one point was dubbed president of my class. That's a story for later.

I intended to cut with my cousin Josh for at least a year before going off on my own. As I look back, my plan was terrible. See, Josh had clients busting out the seams, so I figured when I got out of school, I could catch his overflow while I grew my clients. Nope, it didn't work that way at all. Of course, you know, this industry is built on trust. So, even though I was damn near the mayor, meaning I've never met a stranger, it didn't mean his clients trusted me with their hair. I struggled for about a month at my cousin's shop. It wasn't a financial situation because I had another business, but it didn't help that I was in and out of the shop.

Being inconsistent in a shop is the quickest way to lose your credibility. I learned that the hard way. Also, I was paying rent and utilities for the building that I rented before barberschool. In my mind, I could no longer justify splitting my time and finances between the two.

I had a conversation with Josh, and he encouraged me to do what I thought was best for my situation. He taught me a life lesson in that conversation. He let me know there were enough people in this town for every barber to eat good. I took about a month off from cutting then started working on my shop. I was all-in on the project. I put in, what was at the time, everything in my savings account. Our official grand opening for Valley Cuts Barber and Spa, now Valley Cuts Barbershop, was in March of 2017.

Now, for what seemed like forever before and after we opened, my homeboy Mike bugged me about taking a trip to Charlotte, North Carolina, to meet his mentors. I finally relented, and we planned the trip for that June. See June, for African Americans, is the month we celebrate our Independence Day.

It was June 19, 1865, when Union Soldiers rode into Galveston Texas to let the last of the slaves know they'd been freed, nearly two years after the emancipation proclamation. It was in June of 2017, around the first of the month, that we pulled into Charlotte for a weekend that would change my life.

I saw an organization that blew my mind. I'd never seen a barbershop ran the way the No Grease Barbershops did.

By the time we'd left North Carolina, I'd made my mind to restructure our organization from the bottom up. No Grease gave me the template and inspiration to build something that I believed would be a game-changer for my family, community, and city.

But as the old saying goes, the dream is free, but the hustle is sold separately. Nonetheless, when we got home, I rolled my sleeves up and went to work.

Chapter Two: Let's Talk Business.

In business, you have a few basic models and structures: Sole Proprietors, LLCs, LPs, and General Partnerships. Then there are tax classifications like S Corps and C Corps. There are ways to mix and match those to maximize business potential and profits. But before we get into those, let me introduce you to a concept from Robert Kiyosaki's book, The Cashflow Quadrant. If you're familiar with this book, you may have an idea as to where I'm going with it. For this particular book, there will be a plot twist. There are four categories in the cash flow quadrant. You have the "employee," the "self-employed," the "business owner" and the "investor." For now, I'll skip the "employee."

Mainly, because if you're a barber, then you're familiar with that, and most of you didn't sign up as barbers to be employees. So let's jump to "self-employed."

Most of us joined this industry for the thrill and excitement of self-employment to be our own bosses. The drawback to this idea is, most of us are terrible at being our own boss. I recall scrolling through a Facebook thread in a barber group recently. A new barber asked about the pros and cons of being a barber. One barber replied, the advantages are that you can come and go as you please, and set your own hours. In my opinion, that logic is extremely flawed. Most of your clients, depending on how long you've been a barber, think you're employed by the shop owner. So most of them believe that you're there to work the hours on the door.

At best, with the pro mentioned above to being a barber, you run the risk of looking very inconsistent. Now, if you're an independent contractor, whether booth rent or commission, your shop owner can't legally make you work the shop hours. He or she knows or should know that. The thought here is this; if you are indeed your own boss, you should have and maintain the discipline to work the shop's hours.

Most barbers won't, and I get it. It's simply not what you may have signed up for, and that's ok. This book is for the barber who wants to actually retire before their hands give out on them. Let's move to the "business owner" side of the quadrant. One could make the argument that the barber business and barber industry are two different things.

Hear me out on this one before you disagree. Most sole proprietor-owned shops, meaning most locally ran shops, don't run their shops like the big box barber brands. They have a different structure. The big-box barbers are retail stores with people who happen to cut hair, and they generally pay by the hour with a commission. Most locally-owned shops run their business more like a co-op of sorts. The owner, often time is the person with the most clients, rents the shop. He or she then adds chairs based on the overhead, which in turn offsets the owner's total liability. Yet, the owner is often not in a position to not have to be behind his or her chair. In this regard, you're still technically self-employed and basically own your job, not a business.

That can be a tough pill to swallow, but if you can swallow it, it can be liberating.

Businesses generally come with a system by which you manage, while your system manages your business. Think, Mcdonalds. Their food, for the most part, tastes the same no matter where you go because they have a system. There are several ways you create that system, and it's up to you to be creative in that space.

Excuse me as I use a couple of phrases that I picked up working in a restaurant while in high school, "front of the house" and "back of the house."

As it relates to barbering, let's say the front of the house is the day-to-day cuts, client interaction, and making money. Whereas, the back of the house is everything else it takes to run a well-oiled machine. Your shop budgeting, insurance, sales taxes (if you're selling products), managing utilities, etc.

What I've experienced and learned is this, it's much more advantageous as a shop owner, to build a team and brand that will take care of the front of the house. That leaves you in a position to manage the back-of-the-house operations unhindered.

I've heard it said on many occasions that business owners should be working on the business, not in the business. I think Ray Kroc's famous line, "mind your business" applies here as well. Knowing and understanding the business that you're in goes a long way in how you operate your shop. Hey, if your business is to simply own and run a shop, well, congratulations, you've made it, and this book may not be necessary for you.

But if you're actually in the business of investing, real estate, or something bigger, then you'll want to run your shop/shops to reflect your long-term goal. How do you do that? The answer is simple but not easy; you must begin with the end in mind. What do I mean by that? Take a look at your long-term goals and ask yourself, when I turn 88, where do I want to be in my life? Then ask yourself, what steps can I take right now to get closer to that goal? The more intentional you are in doing that, the clearer your path will be to building a sustainable business system that will manage your shop. An end-game approach to business is a crucial step in the evolution of your business.

In the book Good to Great, Jim Collins sums it up like this "Faith in the end game helps you live through the months or years of build-up." If I May, I'd like to spend a little more time on "The End Game."

Some of the most successful people in business use this approach when making decisions about their business and personal life. Let's take the proverbial funeral eulogy story. If you were to attend your funeral and had a front-row seat to your eulogy, what would be said about your life? Is your current life one worth talking about at your funeral? If not, how can you begin to live that kind of life today? How can you begin to structure your business to reflect that life? My hope is that you'll find a tip or two in this book that will put you on the right course to live the life you deserve both personally and professionally.

Let's talk briefly about the "investor" then circle back around to the "employee", it's about to get interesting. There are shops in the world that aren't owned by barbers at all. Now, until recently, I thought that was kind of dumb. I mean, think about it. Depending on your booth rent or commission rate, multiplied by the number of barbers, minus expenses, and the general undisciplined nature of most barbers, who wants those problems? I made that exact argument to a mentor and shop owner recently. As an investor, he gave me a glimpse as to how to win in that scenario. I won't go into that in this book, but what I will say is this. If you, as an investor, can make that make sense, go for it. It can be of value to other investments. The investment piece I will talk about a little further is, as a barber, what do you do with your money?

Let me explain. One of my favorite gems from Robert Kiyosaki's book, Rich Dad Poor Dad, is the idea of paying yourself first.

In the book, The Richest Man in Babylon, it expands on this principle by saying to pay yourself 10 percent of your gross. So imagine, you make four grand per month.

Your 10 percent would be $400 per month. What do you do with that 10 percent? Let's go a step further. Imagine living beneath your means. How much are your household and personal bills per month? Can you make any cuts in your monthly budget that will add money to that $400 per month? On the surface, you may say, hell no, Chris has lost his mind, and that would be understandable.

But, could you reduce the number of times you go out to eat per month?

Or, could you move certain personal expenses into the business expense column, therefore, saving money? Tom Wheelwright has a great book called Tax Free Wealth, full of dope-ass tax advice that can save money and put you in a position to reinvest. Also, can you sell something that you no longer need?

Can you get rid of an unnecessary expense to save money? My point here is this. If you can create a budget and live beneath it, then you're in a far better position to reinvest your money. Online brokerage companies have introduced "Dollar Based" investing. That means the barrier of entry into the stock market is dumb low.

I can write a whole book on investing alone for barbers, but my goal here is to get you thinking long-term. You can't cut hair forever and you won't cut hair forever.

There's a great book called "I Will Teach You to Be Rich" by Ramit Sethi that's an absolute game-changer on this topic. Now, back to the employee. When I first dipped my toe in the pool of self-employment, it was to be a rapper. Yes, I said it, a rapper, and honestly, I'd like to think I had a pretty good run. Before I turned 20, I'd been to over different 20 states. Rapped in front of thousands of people and met a lot of great people. To this day, I'm still friends with a few people I met during that time. In my hometown, our group was kind of a big deal. As of this writing, I'm 36 and have almost zero to show for my rap career. Yet, I learned a lot from that experience. Like, if you want to sell CDs on your bicycle, make sure you can at least sleep on your best friend's futon. My second venture into self-employment was gold grills. That was an absolute dud.

I bought a grill kit and never made a mold of a single tooth. My third venture was a lot more successful. I decided to start a janitorial company to revive my previous rap career. By this time, I was about 30 years old and thought, this makes complete sense. After every turn of my self-employment journey, my aunt would ask me about things like retirement and backup plans. In my mind, I had a plan, or at least that's what I told myself. And sure, there are things you can do for retirement as a self-employed person, but what happens when you or if you become unemployed? Maybe you saved a few dollars, but how long can you go without working? If you're like me and a lot of other startups, you put your profits back into your "sure thing" with the hopes of saving later. So, you're officially screwed if you are without work. Or, you can punch a clock.

But you're a barber, who the hell wants to punch a clock after being a barber?! That's right, nobody, but it happens. As I thought through the issues of self-employment and unemployment, it hit me. The answer is employment. In general, there aren't many guarantees for someone self-employed, so the goal is to look for and create as many guarantees as possible. Thus, the employment plot twist, but not in the way you'd think. Now, the concepts I'm about to outline may not work for every barber, and you should absolutely talk to your tax professional to see if it fits you. Let me say this too, shop owners, please stop calling your independent contractors, employees. That shit isn't cool, and it could come back to bite you in the ass later. The bottom line is, the IRS has strict guidelines as to the difference between employees and independent contractors. You could very well be blurring that line.

It's important to know if you are or not. If you are, it is smart to take a look at how you're running your shop. With that said, we're off to the races.

Ok, I understand booth renters don't work for the shop owner, but you can still potentially be an employee. Again, I can't emphasize this enough; make sure you talk to a competent tax professional before you try this. Depending on how much you make per year, your tax election, and entity structure, you can easily become your own employee. For example, you could organize yourself as an LLC, elect to be taxed as an S Corp, and you'd be well on your way to being in position for unemployment benefits if you were to be out of work for some time. The LLC could give you some asset protection, and the S Corp could save you some money on your federal taxes.

The next step would be to register your business entity with your state's workforce agency and register your business entity with your state's unemployment insurance office. You'll also need a Tax ID Number (TIN) or Employer Identification Number (EIN), which is basically the same number.

In the case of a Sole Proprietor, that number is usually your Social Security number if you hadn't applied for an EIN. If you form an LLC, it would be wise to apply for your EIN. For asset protection, you and your business must maintain separate identities. Blurring boundaries between you and your business can hurt you in the long term. To apply for your EIN, you'd need to go to the IRS website. It's pretty user-friendly. You should be able to make your S Corp tax election on the same IRS form you filled out for your EIN.

If you're already using an LLC for your shop or to do business with your shop's owner and you're being taxed as a Sole Proprietor, you can still switch to an S Corp using the IRS Tax Form 2553. Your accountant should be able to walk you through it. Taking this route, you'll need a little more discipline over your finances. You'll be required to file and pay fees monthly as well as quarterly payments. You'd also need to pay yearly franchise fees for your LLC, and that cost varies per state.

Shop owners can also benefit from the structure above, especially at a commission-based shop. Not every barber, especially those fresh out of barberschool, has the discipline to save for taxes. As a commission-based shop, in an LLC taxed as an S Corp, you could create a second option for the barbers you bring to your shop.

With the right system in place, you could hire your barbers that are on commission and take the taxes out for them. Instead of giving them a 1099 at the end of the year and them having to deal with the tax burden, they'll get a W2.

As the owner, if you took that approach, the shop would be responsible for supplies. The barbers would still get the flexibility of the contractor without the headache of the accounting.

Check out Garrett Sutton's book, "Rich Dad Advisors: Start Your Own Corporation," and "How to Use Limited Liability Companies and Limited Partnerships." It's also essential that you have separate bank accounts for your personal and business affairs. Realistically, you should already have different bank accounts, but it's even more critical once you start to structure your business correctly.

Transactions should look like this: The money you make from cutting hair goes into your business account, you then should write a check for your salary out of that account, which will go into your personal account for any personal business. All your business transactions should come out of your business account. This will help you during tax time. You may want to look into a third-party payroll service in your city or an app. That adds a layer of accountability, and it makes sure your fees are paid on time. Another key component to better structuring your business is your Operating Agreement. Most banks will require an Operating Agreement along with your state's Articles of Organization before you can open a business banking account. If you don't have an LLC, you can set up a DBA (Doing Business As) account. Some banks may have different names for their business accounts, so you may want to keep that in mind.

Are you still with me? Good, I know that last part was a lot to chew on at one time, if that was the first time you've come across that information. It still makes my head spin. It's also something you'll want to stay on top of because laws change all the time. Now, you may be saying to yourself I don't need to do all of that, I'm in an ok place. Remember the quote right before the introduction? That would apply here. What I'm attempting to outline in the book is the difference between surviving in the barber industry and thriving in the barber business. I've come across business practices, that in the short term, may seem advantageous but, in the long term, are detrimental. Proper business structure, proper bookkeeping, not skimping out on taxes by not reporting income, and adequate money management is a formula for long-term success.

Having good credit is also a crucial component and can be critical to your success, meaning you may not always have cash on hand for specific issues. Having the ability to leverage credit, whether you utilize it or not, is an asset to have in your arsenal. The idea is this; there's no way to work your way into wealth. Have you ever heard the saying, luck is preparation meeting opportunity?

What I've outlined are some things you can do to be prepared for just about any opportunity. You create your own luck with your willingness to do what it takes. So, whether you're entertaining potential investors, looking for a loan to buy a house, build a set of duplexes, or looking for ways to expand your business, if your business affairs are in order, you'll be ready to take on each opportunity. This brings me to my next point —the importance of your team, advisors, and mentors.

Chapter Three: Your Team

There's an old African proverb that says, "If you want to go fast, go alone but if you want to go far, go together." Remember, two heads are better than one. J. Paul Getty once said, "I'd rather have 1% of the effort of 100 men than 100% of my own effort." In short, your job isn't to do everything. The goal should be to do what you excel in and outsource the rest. That's where your advisors come into play. Your advisors, mentors, and team will play a key role in your long-term success, hands down. So let's start with your team. If the plan is to work on your business and not in your business, that means you must recruit for quality, not quantity. Your booth rent needs to be high enough to cover expenses and to make a profit, minus your cutting. It also needs to be fair enough for your barbers to make a living still.

For me, I couldn't wrap my head around high-ass booth rents. How could I charge a barber more than what he or she pays for their rent or mortgage?

On the contrary, I ran a six-figure business before I became a barber, so I couldn't wrap my head around the average booth rent numbers in my area either. So, we chose to go with the commission. Now, I'll be 1000% honest with you; I absolutely hated the idea of a commission. Mike Shelton, co-owner of Uptown Barber Lounge based in Bentonville, Arkansas, was the first shop owner to introduce me to the concept. He then introduced me to the owners and team at No Grease Barbershop in Charlotte, North Carolina; I was sold. It was then that I understood the benefits of running a commission-based shop.

After a weekend with the No Grease team, I not only had the keys to build a great organization, I had the keys to building a functioning business as well. That's when the real work began. When building your team for your shop, think decades, not dollars. How long do you want your shop to survive? These two quotes from Jim Collins' book, Good to Great, captured this theme perfectly. "A company should limit its growth based on its ability to attract enough of the right people" and "Letting the wrong people hang around is unfair to all the right people, as they inevitably find themselves compensating for the inadequacies of the wrong people. Worse, it can drive away the best people. Strong performers are intrinsically motivated by performance, and when they see their efforts impeded by carrying extra weight, they eventually become frustrated."

In short, if you expect to grow your business and grow as a leader, your team is the foundation. If you're not a shop owner, understand this; if your shop is to survive, it's a must that you realize you're the cornerstone of that foundation. Also, understand, depending on your shop's environment, it's far cheaper to see yourself as a partner with the shop's owner than to build a client base and strike out on your own. In some cases, it makes more sense actually to partner with the shop owner and open a second location rather than starting a brand new shop. Let me add this before we move on to the next point. If you're running a booth rent establishment that works for you, by all means, feel free to do business as usual.

If you've been thinking about raising booth rent to cover certain expenses, it may be more advantageous to move in the direction of commission. I know there are shops with a hybrid model that encompasses both. My point in this section is to drive home the importance of building a solid team and making sure you take care of them. To paraphrase the legendary Bridgewater hedge fund manager Ray Dalio, pay your team north of fair. Or, in this case, treat your team north of fair.

Chapter Four: Advisors

Next up are your advisors, or should I say, competent advisors. This part of your team is the next layer of defense and accountability. You should have an accountant, a financial advisor, insurance agents, a lawyer, or at least access to one, and a relationship with your bank.

The accountant. Taxes and tax planning are huge when it comes to long-term success, and if you plan on any growth of any kind, an accountant is essential. And not just any accountant. When I look for an accountant, I'm not just looking for a person with a degree in accounting or someone with that title. I'm looking for someone who knows tax law, who understands the business structure, and who can help me strategize based on those dynamics.

I don't do my own taxes, much like I'd never encouraged my customers to cut their own hair. Also, I don't use tax places that are only open during tax time.

Taxes happen yearly, so I need someone that I can talk to year-round. My suggestion, if you have other business owners as clients, ask them who they'd recommend. Then interview the prospective candidates according to your tax needs. Some accountants also offer bookkeeping. Proper bookkeeping is fundamental. Imagine trying to sell your shop, and a buyer tells you that your shop is worthless. Adequate bookkeeping and a good accountant will make sure your financials are in order and clear. The first accountant I ever used was recommended to me by a previous business partner and associate. The accountant was good but didn't inform me of my sales tax responsibilities. I met my second accountant in a random turn of events.

I was asked to be in a documentary based around the band from my Highschool. Real random, right? You can check out that documentary on YouTube. Search, "Leaving A Legacy Movie." The camera crew and producer's office was right next door to the accountant. Doing that documentary was the best decision I'd make that year. My second accountant gave me so much information and she was also a financial advisor, which fit my long-term goals. The Financial advisor. After you find a good accountant, the next step is the financial advisor. The reason this advisor is second, is that a good accountant should be saving you money. The money you save should be money you invest. A good financial advisor should be able to point you in the right direction based on your long-term financial goals.

Between the accountant and financial advisor, there is a combination of tax-deferred opportunities to save you money and make more money at the same time.

Again, check out Tom Wheelright's book, "Tax-Free Wealth," on this subject.

The insurance agent. An insurance agent can easily be an overlooked component to your team of advisors. Insurance is your first line of defense in asset protection and first-line offense when looking to protect your assets. What do I mean here? Asset protection is twofold. You want to insure the things you think are valuable in case of a loss.

You also want to insure the things you think are valuable in case you're held liable for someone else's losses. When looking into insurance, there are a handful to keep in mind. Also, every person in business, no matter what side of the quadrant you land on, should have life insurance.

A good life insurance policy will not only make sure your family is ok in the event of your death, but it would also help offset any business and personal debts you may owe. It would be a bigger tragedy for your family not only to lose you but to lose your business and possibly your house as well because they can't afford to keep it. A good business liability policy should also be a mandatory component of your plan. Your policy should cover loss or damage to equipment, fire, and medical expenses, to name a few. When you talk to your agent, ask them what they have available for your type of business. Also, you may want to look into accident insurance. In this industry, your hands are your most valuable asset. A good accident insurance policy is key to protecting your assets. Other supplemental plans are available as well with a little homework.

Also, depending on how you set up your business, a shop owner could even provide health insurance for the barbers working his or her shop. The sky is the limit here.

The takeaway here is this; insurance equals assurance. It's nice to have the peace of mind that you're covered in the event of a loss or the loss of someone else. Next up, access to a lawyer. There are times when you will need the help of a lawyer, whether you're selling your shop, acquiring new shops, diversifying interests, or trying to keep someone from taking your money and assets. My Lawyer, Nathan, was a customer in our shop before he became my lawyer. I would listen to the information that he'd give our customers and think if ever need a lawyer, he's who I'm going with. He's definitely been an asset to my long-term estate planning. When rounding out your team of advisors, a relationship with your bank is also key.

Based on your credit and business practices, a relationship with your bank will allow you to have quick access to working capital.

In short, bank loans, buying property, and investing are made so much easier when you have the right team of advisors around you.

Chapter Five: Mentors:

Let's talk about your mentors. I often get asked why I think mentors are an essential part of success. My answer would be, name me one successful sports team without a coach. The right mentor will be your coach. The best mentors bring out the best in the people they coach. So if you're looking to be the best version of yourself, finding a mentor is crucial. I've heard it said when the student is ready, the teacher will appear. Some of the most successful people in the world are people with mentors. Steve Jobs and the founders of Google had Bill Campbell. 50 Cent had Jam Master Jay and Chris Lighty. Bill Gates had Warren Buffet. Socrates mentored Plato, and Plato mentored Aristotle. We can find examples of the mentor/protege relationship throughout history. I've personally had more than a few mentors on my current journey.

In almost every business endeavor, I've found a mentor that has helped me fast-track the learning process and grow both personally and professionally. Now, you may say to yourself, or even to me, finding a mentor is easier said than done. My rebuttal to that would be, finding a mentor is extremely easy. As a matter of fact, the fastest and most efficient way to find a mentor is to pick up a book. Through books and audiobooks, I've found mentors who may never know my name. Yet, the authors in my 250-plus catalog of audiobooks have coached me through business, finance, accounting, taxes, personal growth, and much more. Here's a quick nugget about the mentor/protege relationship. Understand, the mentor/protege dynamic isn't one where the mentor simply pours everything he or she has into the protege.

On the contrary, this relationship is reciprocal. That means it's give and take on both sides of the equation.

My advice in the area of searching for a mentor is to know what value you can bring to that mentor. As a coach and consultant myself, I dread and avoid one-sided relationships. I don't personally believe there is a cookie-cutter template for the mentor/protege relationship. It will vary according to the needs and goals of the relationship. I've even had mentors that have become peers and business partners as the relationships evolved. With that said, good luck on your hunt for a mentor.

Conclusion:

We've all heard the saying, to doing the same thing over again and expect different results is the definition of insanity. I believe we have the opportunity to expand, through barbering, into other arenas and retire comfortably before 65.

Shop owners, imagine you and your barbers owning an apartment complex. Or barbers, imagine you and your coworkers pooling your money for an investment opportunity.

Now, imagine doing so because your bookkeeping, accounting, and taxes are in order. I don't think that can or will happen on a large scale with changing the way we do business, as a whole, internally. Better habits and practices make for better shops. Better shops make for better customers and better barbers working in those shops.

At the time of this writing, according to IBISWorld.com, the barber industry grew 1.8% from 2013 to 2018. Where do you see yourself over the next five years? With the recent resurgence of barbering, I believe we have an opportunity to revolutionize how we do business in this industry. That revolution is what I intended to outline in this book. A Data USA statistic stated the average salary of a male barber was about $29k per year. With the average female barber trailing her male counterpart, making an average of $4k less per year. With that said, I believe there's a lot more room for female barbers. With female barbers making up roughly under 30% of the industry, there's a huge opportunity for greater diversity. In closing, Malcolm X once said, "The future belongs to those who prepare for it today." Barbering has a legacy rooted in the cradle of civilization.

It is one of the oldest and most respected occupations on the globe. I am absolutely proud to be counted amongst this esteemed group of professionals. Thank you for taking the time to check out this book. I wish you nothing but success in your endeavors.

Acknowledgments:

I'd like to say thanks to Josh Enoch, Mike Shelton, and Jesse Soto for encouraging me to go to barberschool. Also, for being my barber brothers, keeping me accountable, and continuing to support my goals. Thank you, Designer Barber and Stylist School, I appreciate the opportunity to go through your program. Thank you to Mr. Dame and Jermaine Johnson and Mr. Charlie Petty for opening my eyes to the potentials of the barber business. Thank you to my Aunt Sue and Uncle Arthur for believing in me even when I sound outlandish. S/o to Jay, Mark, and Paul for keeping sharp and on my toes. S/o to my team of advisors, my lawyer, my accountants, my financial advisors, insurance agents, and friends at the bank. And, I've saved the best for last. I want to extend a huge thank you to our team at Valley Cuts Barbershop.

Without you all, this would be a pipe dream. You dared to believe and walked side by side with me on this journey. I truly appreciate that.

P.S.

A note to my 20-year-old self:

"Dear Chris, you can and you will, if you're willing to do what it takes right now. Remember, all you really have is right now. Nothing else."

Sincerely yours,

Chris, your 36-year-old self.